Elizabeth Cady Stanton

A Photo-Illustrated Biography
by Lucile Davis

Content Consultant:
Andrea Libresco
Department of Curriculum and Teaching
Hofstra University

Bridgestone Books
an imprint of Capstone Press

Facts about Elizabeth Cady Stanton

- Elizabeth Cady Stanton started the struggle for woman suffrage. Suffrage means the right to vote.
- Elizabeth planned the first women's rights convention at Seneca Falls, New York.
- Elizabeth spoke before the U.S. Congress in 1892. She asked Congress to pass a law that would allow women to vote.

Bridgestone Books are published by Capstone Press
818 North Willow Street, Mankato, Minnesota 56001
http://www.capstone-press.com

Printed in the United States of America

Library of Congress Cataloging-in-Publication Data
Davis, Lucile.
Elizabeth Cady Stanton : a photo-illustrated biography / by Lucile Davis.
    p. cm. — (Read and discover photo-illustrated biographies)
  Includes bibliographical references (p. 24).
  Summary: A brief biography of the staunch supporter of women's rights who
helped plan the historic Woman's Rights Convention in Seneca Falls, New York,
in 1848.
  ISBN 1-56065-748-0
  1. Stanton, Elizabeth Cady, 1815-1902—Juvenile literature.
2. Feminists—United States—Biography—Juvenile literature.
3. Women's rights—United States—History—Juvenile literature.
[1. Stanton, Elizabeth Cady, 1815-1902. 2. Feminists. 3. Women—Biography.]
I. Title. II. Series.
HQ1413.S67D38 1998
305.42'092—dc21
[B]   97-41653
                                                                        CIP
                                                                         AC

Editorial Credits
Editor, Greg Linder; cover design, Timothy Halldin; photo research, Michelle L. Norstad

Photo Credits: Archive Photos, cover, 10, 12, 18; Corbis-Bettmann, 4, 16; Johnstown Historical Society, 6; The National Portrait Gallery, Smithsonian Institution, 20; Seneca Falls Historical Society, 14; Sophia Smith Collection, Smith College, 8

Table of Contents

Women's Rights Leader

Elizabeth Cady Stanton worked to gain equal rights for women. A right is something the law allows people to do.

In the 1800s, most women stayed home and raised children. They had few rights. Women could not own property. Women could not vote or sue people in court. They could not attend most colleges. A college is a school people go to after high school.

Men could do all of these things. Laws even gave husbands the right to beat their wives.

Elizabeth started a movement to change unfair laws. A movement is a group of people who support a cause. Elizabeth gave speeches and wrote books about women's rights. She spent more than 50 years working for woman suffrage. Suffrage means the right to vote.

Elizabeth worked to change unfair laws.

Boys Must Be Better

Elizabeth was born November 12, 1815, in Johnstown, New York. Her parents were Daniel and Margaret Cady. Daniel was a lawyer. A lawyer is a person trained in the law. Daniel was also a judge.

There were five girls and one boy in the Cady family. Neighbors came to visit when Elizabeth's youngest sister Catherine was born. They said it was too bad the baby was a girl. This made Elizabeth think boys must be better than girls.

Elizabeth was 11 years old when her brother Eleazar died. Judge Cady was very sad. Elizabeth tried to cheer him up. She promised to act like a son. Her father just shook his head. He said he wished Elizabeth was a boy.

Elizabeth's father was Judge Daniel Cady.

Like Her Brother

Elizabeth decided she would be like her brother. She would be brave. She would learn to ride horses. She would study what boys studied at school.

Elizabeth was the only girl in her class. She won a prize for learning the Greek language. She was sure her father would be proud. But her father said she should have been a boy.

Elizabeth did not stop trying to please Judge Cady. She read her father's law books. She listened as he talked to people about the law. The judge often helped men who had legal troubles. He could not help women because they had few rights. Elizabeth believed that women should have rights, too.

Judge Cady said he could not change New York's laws. Only the state legislature could make the laws more fair. A legislature is a group of people that makes laws.

Elizabeth read her father's law books.

Abolition and Marriage

Elizabeth finished school in 1833. She visited her cousin Libby Smith. Libby's father was an abolitionist. An abolitionist is a person opposed to slavery. Abolitionists believe that no one should own another person. Elizabeth agreed. She decided that laws allowing slavery must be changed.

Elizabeth met an abolitionist named Henry Stanton. Henry asked her to marry him. Elizabeth said yes. Judge Cady did not want them to marry.

Henry planned to attend an anti-slavery meeting in London, England. Elizabeth did not want Henry to go without her. They married in 1840. Then they went to the meeting in London together.

Elizabeth became an abolitionist.

A Meeting in London

Elizabeth met Lucretia Mott in London. Lucretia was an abolitionist from Philadelphia.

Lucretia and Elizabeth were unhappy about the anti-slavery meeting. Women who attended were not allowed to speak. They were not even allowed to sit with the men. Elizabeth and Lucretia knew this was unfair.

Abolitionists wanted slaves to be free. They said slaves should have the same rights as white men. Elizabeth and Lucretia believed that women should also have those rights.

Elizabeth and Lucretia made up their minds. They would hold a meeting for women in the United States. Women would talk about how to gain their rights at this meeting.

Lucretia Mott was an abolitionist from Philadelphia.

On·this·spot·stood·the·Wesleyan·Chapel·
·where·the·First·Woman's·Rights·Convention·
·in·the·World's·history·was·held·
·July·19·and·20·1848·

Elizabeth·Cady·Stanton·
moved·this·resolution·
·which·was·seconded·by·Frederick·Douglass·
"That·it·is·the·duty·of·the·women·
of·this·country·to·secure·to·themselves·
their·sacred·right·
to·the·elective·franchise"

Some·of·the·signers·of·the·Declaration·of·Rights·

Seneca Falls

Elizabeth and Henry returned to New York. They settled in Seneca Falls, New York, and started a family. Henry became a lawyer.

In 1848, Elizabeth and Lucretia Mott met again. They planned a convention. A convention is a meeting for people with the same interests.

The Seneca Falls meeting began on July 19, 1848. It was the first women's rights convention. About 300 men and women attended. Elizabeth helped write a paper called the Declaration of Sentiments. Many people at the meeting signed this paper.

The paper said women should have the same rights as men. It said that women should be able to vote and have jobs. It listed other rights that women at the convention wanted. Elizabeth said the most important one was the right to vote.

The first women's rights convention began on July 19, 1848.

Woman Suffrage

Most men did not want women to vote. But women could not change laws without voting. Elizabeth started a woman suffrage group. The group worked to gain voting rights for women.

Women began holding suffrage meetings throughout New York. Elizabeth spoke at these meetings. Many women asked her to speak to the state legislature. She decided she would do it.

Elizabeth's father was upset. Judge Cady did not believe a woman should speak in public.

Elizabeth worked on her speech for two months. She spoke to the legislature in February 1854. She asked legislators to pass a law allowing women to vote.

The men in the legislature praised her speech. But they did not do what she asked.

This cartoon shows Elizabeth speaking to the New York legislature. She asked the legislature to let women vote.

Speaking and Writing

Elizabeth traveled to many states. She spoke to men and women about woman suffrage. But Elizabeth could not always travel. She and her husband had seven children. Henry was often away from home. Elizabeth stayed home to take care of the children.

Elizabeth had met Susan B. Anthony in 1851. They became friends for life. Elizabeth wrote about women's rights when she could not travel. She also wrote speeches for Susan. Susan was also working hard for women's rights.

Elizabeth wrote articles for a women's newspaper called *The Lily.* She and Susan also started their own newspaper. It was called *The Revolution.* They published this newspaper from 1868 until 1870.

Later, they wrote three books about the woman suffrage movement. The first one was published in 1881. It was called *History of Woman Suffrage.*

Elizabeth and Susan B. Anthony became friends for life.

The 19th Amendment

Elizabeth spoke to the United States Congress in 1892. Congress makes laws for the whole country.

Elizabeth asked for a law that would let women vote. Many congressmen admired her speech. But they did not do what she asked.

Elizabeth wrote to President Theodore Roosevelt on October 25, 1902. She asked him to help women gain the right to vote. Elizabeth died the next day.

On August 26, 1920, Congress passed the 19th Amendment to the Constitution. An amendment is a change in the law. The 19th Amendment gave women the right to vote.

The amendment passed because of the work of many women leaders. Elizabeth Cady Stanton was one of those leaders.

The 19th Amendment passed because of leaders like Elizabeth Cady Stanton.

Words from Elizabeth Cady Stanton

"*Resolved.* That woman is man's equal—was intended to be so by the Creator, and the highest good of the race demands that she should be recognized as such."

From The Declaration of Sentiments

"No matter how much women prefer to lean, to be protected and supported, nor how much men prefer to have them do so, they must make the voyage of life alone."

From a speech entitled "The Solitude of Self"

"Men, their rights and nothing more.
Women, their rights and nothing less."

Motto of *The Revolution,* the newspaper started by Elizabeth and Susan B. Anthony.

Important Dates in Elizabeth Cady Stanton's Life

1815—Born on November 12 in Johnstown, New York
1833—Finishes school
1840—Marries Henry Stanton; attends anti-slavery meeting in London
1840—Meets Lucretia Mott
1848—Arranges the first women's rights convention
1851—Meets Susan B. Anthony
1854—Speaks to New York State Legislature
1881—Publishes *History of Woman Suffrage*
1892—Speaks to the U.S. Congress
1902—Dies on October 26 in New York

Words to Know

abolitionist (ab-uh-LISH-uh-nist)—a person opposed to slavery

college (KOL-ij)—a school people attend after high school

Congress (KONG-griss)—the part of the U.S. government that makes laws for the whole country

convention (kuhn-VEN-shuhn)—a meeting for people with the same interests

lawyer (LAW-yur)—a person trained in the law

legislature (LEJ-iss-lay-chur)—a group of people that makes laws

movement (MOOV-muhnt)—a group of people who support a cause

right (RITE)—something the law allows people to do

suffrage (SUF-ruhj)—the right to vote

Read More

Fritz, Jean. *You Want Women to Vote, Lizzie Stanton?* New York: G.P. Putnam's Sons, 1995.

Harvey, Miles. *Women's Voting Rights*. Cornerstones of Freedom. Danbury, Conn.: Children's Press, 1996.

Johnston, Norma. *Remember the Ladies: The First Women's Rights Convention.* New York: Scholastic, 1995.

McCully, Emily Arnold. *The Ballot Box Battle*. New York: Alfred A. Knopf, 1996.

Useful Addresses and Internet Sites

National Women's Hall of Fame
Director
P.O. Box 335
Seneca Falls, NY 13148

Women's Rights National Historical Park
136 Fall Street
Seneca Falls, NY 13148

Elizabeth Cady Stanton
http://www.nps.gov/wori/ecs.htm
Encyclopedia of Women's History
http://www.teleport.com/~megaines/women.html

Index